SITTIN' IN with the BIG BAND

jazz ensemble play-along

Volume II

Track 1: tune to B♭ concert.

How to Use This Book

Each arrangement has two audio tracks:
1) Demonstration track. The 1st alto saxophone part is in the mix. Listen to how your part is played by professional musicians to copy the phrasing, intonation, articulation, feel, style, section/ensemble blend, and concept.
2) Play-Along track. Your part has been taken out of the mix. You play along with the big band.
3) See page 32 for Performance Notes.
4) There is a two-measure count-off click at the beginning of each play-along track.

Belwin JAZZ
a division of Alfred

alfred.com

Stream or download the audio content for this book. To access online media, visit: **www.alfred.com/redeem**
Enter the following code: **00-30668_992244**

© 2009 Belwin-Mills Publishing Corp.
A Division of Alfred Music
All Rights Reserved Including Public Performance

ISBN-10: 0-7390-5699-9
ISBN-13: 978-0-7390-5699-8

ON GREEN DOLPHIN STREET

1ST Eb ALTO SAXOPHONE

Music by BRONISLAU KAPER
Lyrics by NED WASHINGTON
Arranged by DAVE WOLPE

LA SUERTE DE LOS TONTOS
Fortune of Fools

1st Eb Alto Saxophone

By JOHNNY RICHARDS
Arranged by VICTOR LOPEZ

TROFEO DE BOLOS

By CRAIG SKEFFINGTON

1st Eb Alto Saxophone

JUMP

1st Eb Alto Saxophone

By WYNTON MARSALIS
Arranged by DAVID BERGER

ALIANZA

1st Eb Alto Saxophone

By ERIK MORALES (ASCAP)

This page left blank to assist with page turns.

SECRET LOVE

1st Eb Alto Saxophone

Words by PAUL FRANCIS WEBSTER
Music by SAMMY FAIN
Arranged by GREG YASINITSKY

THE RED DOOR

1st Eb Alto Saxophone

By GERRY MULLIGAN and ZOOT SIMS
Arranged by W. SCOTT RAGSDALE

GREENSLEEVES

1st Eb Alto Saxophone

Traditional
Arranged by GREG YASINITSKY

24

This page left blank to assist with page turns.

SOFTLY, AS IN A MORNING SUNRISE

1st Eb Alto Saxophone

Words by OSCAR HAMMERSTEIN II
Music by SIGMUND ROMBERG
Arranged by DAVE RIVELLO

28

This page left blank to assist with page turns.

GET IT ON

1st Eb Alto Saxophone

Words and Music by BILL CHASE
and TERRY RICHARDS
Arranged by VICTOR LOPEZ

PERFORMANCE NOTES FOR ALTO SAX

Playing the 1st alto chair in a big band is a challenging but very rewarding job. Here are a few tips for playing lead alto in a big band:

- Focus on blend, intonation, articulation, phrasing, and playing with accurate time. In addition, listen to the lead trumpet and match the style, pitch, sound, and feel.
- Don't over-blow on the loud dynamics because it may affect your intonation.
- Listen and fit your part on top of the section harmony.
- In a rock or Latin style chart, the eighth notes are played even, not swung.
- In a rock style arrangement chart, carefully observe the rhythmic syncopation.
- Observe articulations and dynamic markings throughout the charts.
- Make sure you can hear the recording well so you can lock in your time and feel with the band.
- The marcato or rooftop accent (∧) is played detached but not staccato—think "daht."
- Check out each arrangement so you are prepared to handle any awkward page turns or a D.S. and codas.
- Try recording yourself while you play along with the play-along track and see how close you can get to sounding like you are in the band.
- Have fun being the "virtual" lead alto player!

There is a two-measure count-off click at the beginning of each play-along track

On Green Dolphin Street:
1) Play the unison lines in tune—listen to the other saxes and blend. Don't over-blow.
2) For the soli sections, play the written articulation accurately, but don't play the staccatos too short.
3) Play a solo the second time at measure 35—you can play the written solo or ad-lib. Listen and learn from the demo track. Learn the melody and study the chords and scales for the chords.

La Suerte de los Tontos:
1) The 6/8 meter can be tricky—count this chart in "2." Listen to the demo track and observe the rhythmical patterns and groupings in this meter.
2) For the unison lines, listen, blend, and match the intonation of the musicians on the tracks.
3) For the solo at measure 96, try playing the written solo the first time through, then embellish or work on your improvisation on the repeat. Learn the notes of the chords and scales in the solo.

Trofeo de Bolos:
1) In this Latin chart, play the eighth notes even, not swung.
2) Observe the articulation and keep the staccato notes tight and clean.
3) The marcato or rooftop accent (∧) is played detached—think "daht."
4) One of the challenges of this chart is the rhythmic syncopation. Listen, relax, and subdivide!
5) For the solo at measure 53, play the written solo or improvise. Notice that there is a three-chord harmonic pattern that repeats. Learn the notes of the chords and improvise!

Jump:
1) This traditional swing style is concise and tight. Listen closely and match the articulation.
2) The solo at measure 35 can be played as written or improvised, but keep the solo in the style.
3) At measure 99, play the eighth notes legato and at 109, use a light tongue for a "doo, doo, doo" articulation so the eighth notes can swing.
4) Play with authority. The excitement comes from the accents, not from volume. Keep the feel light and drive the swing feel relentlessly.

Alianza:

1) This chart goes between a Latin feel and a swing feel; however, at this tempo, this is not much difference in the eighth-note concept.
2) N.B. refers to "no breath."
3) For the solo break at measure 63, focus on playing with accurate time—always practice with a metronome. The solo can be played as written or improvised. Listen to the chord progression as you study and learn the chords.
4) Right after the solo there is a sax soli for a few measures. Dig in and lead the section!
5) Observe the dynamics.

Secret Love:

1) The marcato or rooftop accent (∧) is played detached—think "daht."
2) Play this chart with a solid swing feel. Listen to the demo track for the swing concept.
3) At measure 59, the saxes have a nice soli. Lead the section, but listen and blend. At measure 81, the rhythm section is out, so focus on maintaining accurate time for the section.
4) The tempo is much slower at the ending of the chart—listen carefully.

The Red Door:

1) Observe the key signature! Play with a solid and full sound on measure 1, but in tune.
2) The unison at measure 9 has some tricky fingerings for the alto—watch out for the low C-sharp to B transition. Work on that fingering so it sounds smooth.
3) This chart has a relaxed swing feel—listen to the demo and copy the style.
4) Play the solo at measure 39 as written or improvise.
5) Dig into the sax soli beginning in measure 73. Keep it relaxed and swingin'. Careful of the page turns and the D.S. al coda.

Greensleeves:

1) This chart changes meters. Beginning as a jazz waltz, at measure 89 it goes into a 4/4 swing, then back to the waltz at 133.
2) The waltz section should have a nice smooth flow to the phrasing. Observe the dynamics.
3) The marcato or rooftop accent (∧) is played detached—think "daht."
4) Play the solo at measure 105 as written or improvise. Learning the notes in the chords and scales will help you navigate through the chord progression.

Softly, As in a Morning Sunrise:

1) This chart fluctuates between Latin and swing feel. Keep in mind that eighth notes are played even in Latin music.
2) The solo can be played as written or improvised. Learn the melody from memory, then study the notes in the chords to help improve your improvisation.
3) The swing-feel sax soli comes right out of a drum solo in measure 111, so listen and count.
4) Watch out for the page turns and the D.S. al coda.

Get it On:

1) Play the eighth notes even in a rock-feel chart.
2) Watch out for the syncopated rhythms and observe the articulation carefully. Accuracy is critical.
3) The sections at measures 43 and 65 are legato.
4) The drums set the tempo in measure 75.

Recorded at **Bias Recording Studios**, Springfield, VA
Bob Dawson, Engineer
Featuring the **Belwin Jazz Big Band, Pete BarenBregge**, Director.